BRAVE KIDS

Cora Frear

A true story

BRAVE KIDS

Cora Frear

A true story

Susan E. Goodman
Illustrated by Doris Ettlinger

Aladdin Paperbacks
New York London Toronto Sydney Singapore

First Aladdin edition March 2002
Text copyright © 2002 by Susan E. Goodman
Illustrations copyright © 2002 by Doris Ettlinger

Aladdin Paperbacks
An imprint of Simon & Schuster
Children's Publishing Division
1230 Avenue of the Americas
New York, NY 10020

Designed by Lisa Vega
The text of this book was set in Palatino
Printed and bound in the United States of America

10 9 8 7 6

Library of Congress Cataloging-in-Publication Data
Goodman, Susan E. 1952–
Cora Frear: a true story / Susan E. Goodman ; illustrated by Doris Ettlinger—
1st ed.
p. cm.
Summary: While making house calls with her frontier-doctor father, Cora Frear finds herself in a dangerous situation as she and her father are surrounded by a prairie fire raging out of control.
ISBN-13: 978-0-689-84329-7 (ISBN-10: 0-689-84329-1) (Aladdin pbk.)
ISBN-13: 978-0-689-84330-3 (ISBN-10: 0-689-84330-5) (library ed.)
[1. Frear, Cora, 1887-1985—Childhood and youth—Juvenile literature. 2. Pioneer children—Iowa—Biography—Juvenile literature. 3. Frontier and pioneer life—Iowa—Juvenile literature.]
Brave Kids/Ready-for-chapters
2002511855

0110 OFF

To Mom, also a hero

Acknowledgments:

Thanks to Michael Smith who introduced me to Cora, Doris E. Ettlinger who has brought her alive in pictures, and to Dawn Chapman at Dorothy Pecaut Nature Center who helped make sure the prairie I described was the one Cora loved so well. Marjorie Waters, Janet Coleman, Lisa Jahn-Clough, and Liza Ketchum were great readers as always. And a special thanks to Ellen Krieger, who has been wonderful every step of the way.

Table of Contents

Chapter One

Papa's Best Assistant

Cora woke to the sound of Mamma grinding the coffee beans. Morning already. Cora pulled her blanket over her head. She snuggled into her pillow.

Soon Cora heard the oatmeal pot clang onto the stove. She got up and went to her parents' bedroom. She climbed onto the bed and bounced a little. Then, a little more.

Papa opened one eye. He reached out and gave Cora a good-morning hug. "Carrie," he said, using Cora's special nickname, "I might look in on Albert Ralston. I need to see how his ankle is healing. Do you want to come to work with me this afternoon?"

"Of course I do," Cora answered. She smiled. Suddenly, an ordinary day had turned into an adventure.

"I'm glad you're coming," Papa said. "You never know when I'll need my best assistant."

Cora's father was Doc Frear. He was doctor to the town of Sloan, Iowa, and the neighboring countryside. Many of his patients lived on farms, far out on the prairie. Sometimes they could not come into town to see him. Then Doc Frear would climb in his buggy and make a house call.

Whenever she could, Cora went along. She loved riding through the prairie. She loved meeting the new families moving in to settle Iowa's wilderness. They came from Sweden and Norway, Ireland and Germany. Their homes were filled with bright quilts, furniture painted with flowers, and cookies flavored with unusual spices like pepper. Visiting these houses was like taking a trip across the ocean.

Most of all, Cora loved helping Papa. It was always exciting. When they made house calls, Cora often baby-sat for the young children. That way, their mother had a chance to be alone with the doctor.

But sometimes Cora was a real assistant. At ten years old, she knew how to chloroform patients so they would sleep when Papa needed to operate.

Cora came home from Sunday School at noon. The horses were hitched to the buggy.

Papa was waiting. "Mamma set out some lunch for you," Papa said. "Eat quickly. Then we're off to the Ralstons'."

Cora ran into the house. She plunked herself down at the kitchen table. She put some wild plum butter on Mamma's freshly baked bread. Then she took a huge bite. Before she even had a chance to chew, she took another.

"Take off your coat," Mamma said, stirring a pot on the stove. "And your bonnet."

How does she do that? Her back is turned, Cora thought. *Does she have eyes in the back of her head?*

Cora took off her coat and her bonnet. She threw them on a chair. Then she gulped down her milk.

Mamma walked over to Cora and smiled. She reached down and gently tugged Cora's short brown braids. "Slow down, Cora. He'll

wait for you," Mamma said. "He always does."

After lunch, Mamma insisted that Cora wear her heavy coat. She made Cora wear her red velvet bonnet, even her long underwear. When Cora climbed into the buggy, Papa tucked a blanket around her knees.

"It's not *that* cold," Cora said.

"You know what happens in September," he answered. "There will be a strong wind blowing across the prairie."

Cora peeked in the back of the buggy. She looked again. "I don't see your medicine bag, Papa," she said. "You didn't forget it, did you?"

Papa smiled at Cora. As he walked to his side of the buggy, he patted the big black box in back. "I put it in the trunk," he said.

"Doctor Frear! Doctor Frear!" a voice called out.

Cora and her father looked up. A wagon was pulling up to their gate. A man handed the reins to his wife. He jumped down and started up the walk. Papa went to meet him halfway.

It didn't take long before the man turned back to his buckboard. He drove on toward Sloan as Papa climbed up next to Cora.

"We have a message from the prairie. Looks like Albert's ankle will have to wait," Papa told her. "We're off to the hills. The Miller baby is running a fever."

Chapter Two

Out on the Prairie

"Giddy-up, Jim," Papa said, flicking the reins. "Giddy-up, Baldy."

Old Jim and Baldy looked odd walking together. Jim was a big chestnut brown horse. Baldy was a smaller tan one. But they made a good team.

It didn't take long for the horses to trot past Sloan's main street. Gradually, the houses grew farther and farther apart. Soon, there were no houses at all. The horses slowed to a walk. They plodded down the country lane.

"Papa, don't we have to hurry?" asked Cora. "What about the baby?"

"Don't worry. I think the baby will be fine," he answered. "A lot of children have been getting fevers and stomachaches this fall. We just have to make sure that it's nothing more serious."

Finally, they reached the beginning of the prairie. Papa guided Jim and Baldy off the road. The horses carefully walked down the steep bank.

Will the buggy tip over? Cora thought. It never did, but Cora was always nervous about it. She pretended she wasn't afraid. But she gripped the side of her seat until they were on the wide, flat prairie.

The horses stepped onto a wagon trail, two deep ruts made by wheels and hoofs. The grass rose up tall all around them. In many places, it towered over the buggy.

Cora loved the prairie colors in fall. The grass was a waving sea of gold and rust. Elderberry bushes added splashes of red. Wildflowers like goldenrod and blazing star dotted the prairie with yellow and purple.

"Listen to the bobwhite, Papa," said Cora.

"M-o-r-e wet," the bird cried. "M-o-r-e wet."

"He's right," Papa said, smiling at his own joke. "We sure could use more rain. It's so dry this year."

That was the last thing either of them said for a long time. Instead, they listened to the rattle of the buggy. And the rhythm of the horses' hooves. And the music of the grass rustling in the wind.

Cora watched a jackrabbit hop alongside them for a moment. Then it dashed out of sight. She smiled and nudged her father. "Look, Papa," she said, "we're not the only ones out on a Sunday afternoon."

Suddenly the buggy jolted and started to go faster. Cora looked at the horses. Both of them had pushed their noses forward. Jim's ears were flat against his head.

A frightened meadowlark shot up out of the grass. The bird managed to scare Jim and Baldy a little, too. They started to trot.

"The horses must be tired of walking," said Papa. He tightened his hold on the reins.

Cora watched another meadowlark fly off with a frightened cry. She saw a cottontail rabbit hop by. Then a prairie chicken began to squawk.

"Why are Jim and Baldy running? And what about all the other animals?" Cora asked. "They look like they're afraid of something."

Cora pulled herself out of the seat. She looked back over the buggy. She stared at the prairie behind them. She almost expected to see a wolf charging out from the tall grass. Or a bobcat ready to leap onto the buggy.

But everything was still.

"Well, *something* is wrong. Old Jim and Baldy sure know it," said Papa.

Cora looked at the horses. Jim and Baldy were snorting and tossing their heads. Papa tried to distract them by jiggling the bits in their mouths with the reins. "The wind is picking up," he said. "Maybe we're going to have a storm."

Cora looked at the blue sky in front of them. No clouds in sight. Then she glanced in back of them again. This time she looked at the sky instead of the waving grass. "I think you're right, Papa," she said. "There are some funny-looking clouds right behind us."

Papa didn't turn around. He couldn't. Jim and Baldy were trying to break into a run. Papa was working very hard to rein them in.

So Cora looked again. This time, she didn't think those clouds looked funny at all.

The clouds looked dark and angry. They were growing bigger and bigger. They were still far in the distance. But, they were getting closer every second.

Now Cora could see a red glow in the sky. "It's a prairie fire!" she shouted. "Papa, we'll be burned alive!"

Chapter Three

Prairie Fire!

Cora had heard about prairie fires. Everyone in Iowa knew about them. These walls of flame raced across the prairie as fast as the wind.

"Papa, what do we do?" Cora cried.

Cora looked at her father. She almost wished she hadn't. Papa usually had the answers to all of her problems. This time, Papa didn't say a word. Instead, he was gripping the reins very hard, even though the horses were under control.

A prairie fire! Prairie grass was thick. In the fall, it turned brown. When there wasn't much rain, the grass was as dry as old newspaper. All it took to start a fire was a bolt of lightning hitting the ground. Or one spark from a hunter's gun. Or a coal from the campfire of a careless traveler.

In minutes, a single flame could grow into a raging blaze. The prairie had no trees to slow a fire down. People said that a fire could sweep over the prairie like a racehorse.

Cora looked at their old farm horses. Their noses were already twitching with the first whiff of smoke. She could see Old Jim's eyes opening wide. Baldy was beginning to pant.

Jim and Baldy could never outrun the fire. They were miles away from the road, anyway. They were too far from the edge of the prairie to escape in time.

"Oh, Papa," Cora said.

She didn't say anything else. She couldn't. If she opened her mouth again, she would start to cry.

"Don't fret, Carrie," he said. "We are going to be all right."

He doesn't sound so sure of that, Cora thought. She started to get even more frightened.

Then she made the voice inside her head sound like a scolding schoolteacher. *Cora Frear,* it said, *he is your father. He has always taken good care of you. It will be the same today.*

"All right, Papa," Cora said quietly. "What can I do to help?"

Papa stopped the horses. He looked all around him. He watched the way the wind was blowing. "Get out of the buggy," he said. "I'm going to move the horses."

Papa jumped out of the buggy, too. He grabbed the reins and led the horses to one side of the trail. He quietly stroked Jim and Baldy until they were calm.

Papa hurried to the other side of the trail. He picked the driest grass he could find. He put it all in a little pile. "Cora, get the blanket you were using. Bring it over here," he said.

Cora got the blanket out of the wagon. She ran to Papa. She watched him kneel on the ground.

"We're going to make our own fire," said Papa.

"Why?" Cora asked. *Isn't one dangerous enough?* she thought.

"Our fire will burn the grass near us," Papa explained. "It will leave a big spot for us to stand in. When the prairie fire arrives, we will be safe. It will go around us. The

prairie fire cannot burn grass that is already reduced to smoke and ash."

Papa finished making his pile of dried grass. "We're making what they call a 'backfire,'" he said. "But we will call it our 'blessed island of safety.'"

"What about Jim and Baldy?" Cora asked.

"We'll all huddle in there together when the time comes," Papa said. "But while the backfire is burning, we have to make sure it doesn't jump the trail. We can't let it get near the horses."

Papa reached into his pocket. Papa wasn't a smoker. But still he sometimes carried matches. A doctor often had to light his buggy's lantern to go on nighttime calls.

Cora held her breath.

"Got it!" Papa said. He pulled a match from his pocket and waved it in the air.

Papa got as close to the pile of grass as he could. His hand shook a little as he struck the match on the sole of his boot.

Nothing.

He tried again.

Nothing. The match would not light.

"Oh no," Papa said with a moan.

Cora watched Papa bury his face in his hands. That's when she realized he had only one match.

Chapter Four

The Last Match

What are we going to do? How will we survive?
Cora thought.

Cora felt as if she couldn't breathe. She knew that if she asked Papa these questions, he would not have answers.

Suddenly Cora thought of one herself. "Papa, your old vest," she said. "I saw it in the trunk the other day!"

A look of hope flashed in Papa's eyes. "Go get it, Cora," he shouted. "Go quickly!"

Cora didn't need to be told twice. She flew

to the back of the buggy. She opened the trunk and grabbed the vest. On her way back, she began to search through its pockets.

"Have you found a match?" Papa asked.

"Not yet," said Cora.

She reached into another pocket. She pulled out one of Papa's handkerchiefs. She pulled out an old penknife. No matches.

Cora reached into the vest's third and last pocket. This was the little one where men usually kept their watches. Papa didn't have a spare watch to keep in his old vest. Finally, Cora felt something straight and wooden. "A match!" she said happily.

Cora handed the match—the single match—to her father.

Papa knelt down one more time. This time, Cora leaned over him. She spread her skirt wide to block the wind.

"Good luck, Papa," she whispered.

Papa struck the match on his boot. A tiny flame leaped up. Papa quickly laid the match on the pile of grass.

Cora heard a crackling sound. She saw the tiny fire lick at the grass in Papa's pile. Suddenly flames shot up to the sky. Papa barely had a chance to pull Cora back before the fire jumped to the surrounding grass.

The blaze grew. It fanned out, leaping hot and high in the wind.

I wonder if we have just made more trouble for ourselves? Cora thought.

Papa took hold of the blanket. He started beating the flames that came close to the trail.

"Papa," Cora cried, "have we just started our own prairie fire?"

"Take the vest and help me," he shouted.

"We don't care about the fire that is moving away from us. But we must keep the rest of it away from the horses."

Cora stood on the trail. She used the old vest to beat the flames that crept near her. She beat until her arms felt as if they were breaking. Then she kept on beating.

Cora wanted to turn around to look at the real prairie fire. She wanted to see how close it was. But she knew she didn't have time. She kept on beating.

Suddenly Jim's whinny turned into a shriek. A piece of burning grass caught the wind and floated his way. Baldy began to stamp his feet as if he was ready to stomp it out. Instead, Papa rushed over and put out the flame—just as it landed.

"Whoa, Jim. Whoa, Baldy. Stay calm, you two," said Papa. He tried to use as calm and comforting a voice as he could. But he was panting from working so hard.

Take that. And that, Cora thought as she attacked the flames that leaped across the path. She was getting very tired. But she kept on fighting the fire. She knew she was saving Old Jim and Baldy. She knew she was fighting for Papa—and for her own life, as well.

At last, their fire was under control. Cora stared at the patch of burned prairie that they had worked so hard to make. Just minutes before, it had been filled with beautiful swaying grass. It had had golden sunflowers and silvery prairie sage. Now it was black and smoking.

Cora bit her tongue to stop her tears. This was no time to cry. They were safe for the moment. "What do we do now?" she asked.

Papa finished putting out the last little

spits of fire close by. He stood up and dropped the blanket. He wiped the sweat off his face. "We must wait until it cools," he said. "Then we will get in the buggy. And we will drive Old Jim and Baldy into our 'blessed island of safety.'"

Chapter Five

The Island of Safety

The clouds of black and gray rolled closer and closer. They began to block out the sun. The sky looked as it did at twilight instead of the afternoon.

Cora already had the taste of smoke in her mouth from the backfire. She watched the prairie fire coming. She thought about what it would be like to be drowning in smoke. "Is it time yet, Papa?" she asked. "Can we get onto our island now?"

"Not yet, my girl," he answered.

"Are you sure?" she insisted. "The fire is getting so close."

"The ground is still hot, Cora," Papa said. "If we went in now, our horses might get burned."

Papa's voice was quiet, but Cora felt as if she had been scolded.

Does Papa think I am being selfish? she wondered. *Does he think I don't care about Old Jim and Baldy?*

Finally the ground was cool enough. Papa got in the buggy. He took up the reins once more and drove into the blackened prairie.

Papa jumped down to stand between the horses. Jim's eyes were opened very wide. Cora could see the white all around them. Baldy kept tossing his head. Papa pet Jim right between those scared eyes. He scratched Baldy on his favorite spot near his ear. "Don't worry, boys," he said. "We are going to be fine."

Jim and Baldy are trying to listen, thought Cora. *I will, too.*

The harsh smell of smoke grew stronger.

The wall of flames kept getting closer. Cora could see it stretching high above the tall grass in the distance. Her eyes began to sting. Her throat began to burn.

Cora could not take her eyes off the approaching fire.

"There's no more time, Cora," Papa called out. "You need to stand with me between the horses. Right now!"

Papa was right. By the time Cora got to his side, the smoke was getting very thick. Waves of it were sweeping over them. Cora could barely see. She began to cough. "It's hard to breathe," she said.

"This will help all of us," Papa said. He held the blanket so it covered all of their heads.

The wall of flames kept getting closer.

The blanket helped. But as the fire came near, the smoke got thicker than ever. Even under cover, Cora was breathing smoke into her nose and lungs.

The blanket helped shield them from the smoke. But it couldn't help them with the heat.

"It's so hot," Cora whispered. "I feel like a loaf of bread cooking in the oven."

"It's not quite that hot. We'll just end up being half-baked," Papa said, joking to make her feel better.

Cora could hear the air snap and crackle. Pop, pop, popping noises exploded in the air. Now and then, a pop was so loud, it sounded like a rifle shot. The panting of the horses was almost as loud.

The fire was burning around them. The temperature was almost unbearable. The heat seemed to last forever.

Slowly, it began to feel a little cooler. Cora felt as if she had escaped from the oven. Her skin no longer felt as if it were on fire.

The smoke was still thick. But she could breathe again.

Papa took one peek out from under the blanket. Then he lowered his arms so he could look around.

The prairie fire had passed by. They had all made it through alive!

Cora and Papa brushed the last bits of burning grass off the top of the buggy. They shook out the blanket. Cora put her finger in a hole made by some sparks. "This blanket doesn't look so good," she said.

She turned to look at Papa. A drop of

sweat ran down his cheek. It left a clean streak on his face, which was as black as coal, as black as smoke. "You don't look so good, either, Papa," she said.

Papa looked up. The expression on his face was Cora's mirror. She could tell that she was covered with black soot, too. Her face was just as dirty as his.

Cora and Papa stared at each other. Then they laughed as if they had just heard the funniest joke in the world.

Chapter Six

Nature's Way

"The Addison farm is only a few miles away," Papa said, once he stopped laughing. "We can wash up there. A cool drink of water will really hit the spot, won't it?" he added.

After all this, Papa isn't turning around to go home? Cora thought. "I want to see Mamma," she said.

Papa smiled at Cora. He gently pushed her tangled hair back from her face. "I do, too," he said, "but we must keep going. We may be needed now more than ever."

Papa turned the horses to the north. They set off across the blackened prairie.

"The Miller baby still needs tending," said Papa. "And think of all the families that live in the fire's path. They probably protected their houses by making backfires, just like us. But somebody might have gotten hurt."

Cora didn't want to think about those families. She stared straight ahead. She wiped her eyes with her sleeve. Now that it was all over, she felt more scared than before.

Papa glanced over at Cora. "I know you were frightened back there," he said. "So was I."

He reached over and took Cora's hand. "No shame in being scared, Carrie," he said. "It's fine, as long as it doesn't stop you from doing what you need to do. And it didn't stop you or me, did it?"

Cora didn't say a word. She just nodded.

"You found that match," said Papa. "You helped me make the fire. Then you helped me put it out. We saved the horses—and we saved ourselves. We may have been frightened, but I'd say we were pretty brave, too!"

For a while, Cora and Papa rode along without saying a word. Cora listened to the clip-clop of Jim and Baldy's footsteps. Papa held her hand.

"Papa, I prayed when you struck that last match," Cora said finally.

"I'm glad you did," he answered. "That match saved our lives."

As Old Jim and Baldy turned into her lane, Mrs. Addison flew out her front door. "Doctor Frear, thank goodness you're here," she said. "Tom is horribly sick."

Tom Addison had suffered a mild heart attack when the fire came to his place. He was only the first person Papa treated that day. One man had burned his hands while fighting the fire. A woman had gotten so scared, she'd needed some medicine to help her calm down.

Then there was the Miller baby. He did have the same fever that many other children had. Papa told his parents to wash him down with cool water. He gave the baby castor oil to clean out his insides.

By the time Cora and Papa started back, it was nearly sunset. When they got close to the fields of burned grass, Cora tried not to look. Suddenly she realized that Papa was not going to take the main road home. He planned to go across the ruins that used to be Cora's beloved prairie. "Do we have to go this way?" asked Cora. "How will we ever find the trail?"

"We took care of Jim and Baldy earlier today," said Papa. "Now they will take care of us.

"Once, they brought me across the prairie during a blizzard," Papa continued. "All I could see was a solid wall of white snow. If the horses knew where to go then, they can find their way home tonight."

Papa relaxed his hold on the reins. Sure enough, Old Jim and Baldy lumbered on.

How do they know where to go? Cora wondered. *They have nothing to steer by. Everything looks the same—black.*

When the wind blew, ashes filled the air, making the night even darker. Cora thought about the rippling world of grass that had been there just hours before. She felt as if they were the only living things in this horrible, dead world.

Cora's precious prairie was gone.

Cora wanted to ask a question, even though she was afraid to hear the answer. She waited and waited. Finally, it burst out of her. "Will the prairie ever come back?" she asked. "Will it ever be the same?"

"Yes, Carrie," Papa said. "It is Nature's way. Prairie plants have deep roots that weren't even touched by the fire. Next spring, we will take this same ride. And we will see new green grass and—"

"Will there be bird's-foot violets?" Cora broke in. "Will there be Indian apples?"

"Yes, all the early wildflowers," Papa said, smiling. "Later in the summer, the grasses will grow tall. Their seed-heads will whisper in the wind overhead. The golden sunflowers and purple asters will bloom again."

"What about all the animals?" Cora asked.

"Believe it or not, most of them survived the fire," said Papa. "The badgers and ground squirrels went underground into their burrows. Many of the birds just flew away.

"During next year's ride, the meadowlarks will be singing," said Papa. "The mother prairie chickens will scold you when you come too close to their nests. The fox, the fawns—they will be here."

Cora let out a deep breath that she didn't even know she was holding. Finally, she could relax. She leaned against Papa. Half asleep, she listened to the music of the horses clip-clopping their way home.

Cora Frear Hawkins, 1887-1985

This is a true story.

Cora Frear was a real girl, born in 1887. Her father, Edwin D. Frear, was a country doctor in the wide-open prairie of Iowa. Cora and her father really went out to visit a patient and got caught in a prairie fire. Cora really found one—only one—match in her father's old vest. They really made an island of safety that saved their lives.

Cora wrote a book about her childhood. It was called *Buggies, Blizzards, and Babies.*

That's how we know her story. As the author of *Cora Frear*, I added a few things to Cora's account of her adventure on the prairie. I did not always know Cora's private thoughts or conversations, for example. So I imagined a few of them.

We do know, however, that Cora loved working with her father. She used to make bandages for him from old sheets. She kept his instruments clean and free of rust. Other times, she actually helped him practice medicine. As said before, Cora was an expert at putting patients to sleep before an operation. She could also set broken bones all by herself.

Dr. Frear was very proud of Cora. He loved working with her. Yet he never encouraged her to become a doctor. In those days, most people thought doctoring was a man's job. In fact, Dr. Frear often wished Cora were a boy so she could practice medicine with him.

Ideas about what women should do were different in those days. Doctoring was different, too. Doctors didn't have stethoscopes to listen to people's hearts. They didn't have shots that prevented certain diseases. Or medicines that cured other ones.

In those days, doctors often visited sick people in their homes. So frontier doctors spent a lot of time in their buggies. They could be called at two in the morning. They could be called during a blizzard. But these doctors would drive hours—day or night—to see a patient.

A doctor could walk through the door to find a woman having a baby. Somebody could have a dangerous disease. Someone could have an infected gunshot wound. With just a few instruments and medicines the doctor had to handle any problem. Many doctors performed operations on kitchen tables, with no one to help them.

Doctoring was hard. So was life on the prairie. With no trees around, many pioneers built their houses out of mud blocks. The dirt ceilings leaked whenever it rained. Hailstorms could pound crops to pieces in minutes. Swarms of grasshoppers could come and eat everything in sight.

Of course, nothing was more harmful than a prairie fire. Flames crossed the prairie in a solid wall. Sometimes this wall was twenty feet high. The fires usually traveled until they reached a river or stream they could not cross. Then they would die out.

Farmers would plow ditches around their

buildings. They hoped the fire could not jump over these furrows. Sometimes farmers set their own backfires, like Cora's island of safety. They blocked a prairie fire from certain places by using up its fuel.

When Cora was a little girl, most of Iowa was still prairie. This grassland stretched endlessly in every direction. Its flowery grasses grew up to twelve feet high. It was thick enough to hide a herd of cattle. Pioneers who came to the prairie said it made them feel very, very small.

Cora grew up and went to college nearby. At one point, she did think about being a doctor's assistant. She ended up teaching school for a year. Then she got married and raised two children.

Cora Frear Hawkins (her married name) died in 1985. Many changes took place during the ninety-eight years she was alive. By 1985, about half of the doctors in the United States were women. Doctors had amazing tools like antibiotics to fight illness. They used cars to get around instead of buggies. And, they had pretty much stopped making house calls.

Many changes took place in Iowa, too. Today, a big highway runs past Cora's old hometown of Sloan. If you were to go there, you would not see the prairie from your car window. You would see field after field of corn and soybeans. There is barely any prairie left in Iowa. But the sky—and the land—still feel like they will go on forever.

Further Reading

If you liked reading about Cora, the prairie, and pioneer life, you can also try:

Goodman, Susan E. *Ultimate Field Trip 4: A Week in the 1800s.* New York, NY: Atheneum, 2000.

Greenwood, Barbara. *A Pioneer Sampler.* New York: Ticknor & Fields, 1995.

Ketchum, Liza. *Orphan Journey Home.* New York: Avon, 2000.

MacLachlan, Patricia. *Sarah, Plain and Tall.* New York: HarperTrophy, 1987.

Warren, Andrea. *Pioneer Girl: Growing Up on the Prairie.* New York: HarperCollins, 1998.

Wilder, Laura Ingalls. *The Little House Books.* New York: HarperCollins.

THE
UNICORN'S SECRET

Experience the Magic

When the battered mare Heart Trilby takes in presents her with a silvery white foal, Heart's life is transformed into one of danger, wonder, and miracles beyond her wildest imaginings. Read about Heart's thrilling quest in

Ready-for-Chapters

THE
UNICORN'S SECRET
Moonsilver
Introducing
The Unicorn's Secret Series

by Kathleen Duey
Illustrated by Omar Rayyan

ALADDIN PAPERBACKS
Simon & Schuster Children's Publishing Division • www.SimonSaysKids.com

apters

MARGARET PETERSON HADDIX

the GIRL with 500 middle NAMES

JANIE WHO?

It's hard enough being the **new** kid in school. It's even **tougher** when all of your new classmates live in big houses and wear expensive **clothes**, while your parents have little and are risking everything just to give you a chance at a better life.

Now Janie's about to do something that will make her stand out even more among the rich **kids** at Satterthwaite School. Something that will have everyone **wondering** just who Janie Sams really is. And something that will mean totally unexpected changes for Janie and her **family**.

ALADDIN PAPERBACKS
Simon & Schuster Children's Publishing • www.SimonSaysKids.com

Read for Chapters